Growing in Grace
The Practice of
Intentional Faith Development

Robert Schnase

ABINGDON PRESS
Nashville

Growing in Grace:
The Practice of Intentional Faith Development
Copyright © 2010, 2014 by Robert Schnase

All rights reserved.

Originally appeared in *Five Practices of Fruitful Living* by Robert Schnase,
which was published by Abingdon Press in 2010.

ISBN 978-1-6308-8302-7

All Scripture quotations, unless otherwise indicated, are taken from the
New Revised Standard Version of the Bible, copyright 1989, Division of
Christian Education of the National Council of the Churches of Christ in the
United States of America. Used by permission. All rights reserved.

Scripture quotations noted (*The Message*) are from THE MESSAGE.
Copyright © by Eugene H. Peterson 1993, 1994, 1995, 1996, 2000, 2001, 2002.
Used by permission of NavPress Publishing Group.

14 15 16 17 18 19 20 21 22 23--10 9 8 7 6 5 4 3 2 1
MANUFACTURED IN THE UNITED STATES OF AMERICA

Contents

Growing in Grace
The Practice of
Intentional Faith Development

Let us consider how to provoke one another to love and good deeds, not neglecting to meet together, as is the habit of some, but encouraging one another . . .

—Hebrews 10:24-25

The Fruitful Living Series

Jesus taught a way of life and invited people into a relationship with God that was vibrant, dynamic, and fruitful. He said, "I am the vine, you are the branches. Those who abide in me and I in them bear much fruit…. My father is glorified by this, that you bear much fruit and become my disciples," (John 15: 5, 8) Jesus wanted people to flourish.

Scripture is sprinkled with phrases that point to fruitful living—the kingdom of God, eternal life, immeasurable riches, a peace that passes all understanding, abundant life.

How do I cultivate a life that is abundant, fruitful, purposeful, and deep? What are the commitments, critical risks, and practices that open me to God's transforming grace and that help me discover the difference God intends for me to make in the world?

How do I live the fruitful, flourishing life of a follower of Christ?

Radical Hospitality. Passionate Worship. Intentional Faith Development. Risk-Taking Mission and Service. Extravagant Generosity.

Since the publication of *Five Practices of Fruitful Congregations,* these edgy, provocative, dangerous words have helped hundreds of congregations understand their mission, renew ministries, and stretch toward fruitfulness and excellence for the purposes of Christ.

The Fruitful Living Series moves the discussion of Christian practice from the congregational level to the personal practices of discipleship. The fruitful God-related life develops with intentional and repeated attention to five essential practices that are critical for our growth in Christ.

Radical Hospitality in our personal walk with Christ begins with an extraordinary receptivity to the grace of God. In distinctive and personal ways, we invite God into our hearts and make space for God in our lives. We receive God's love and offer it to others.

Through the practice of *Passionate Worship*, we learn to love God in return. We practice listening to God, allowing God to shape our hearts and minds through prayer, personal devotion, and community worship. We love God.

Through the practice of *Intentional Faith Development,* we do the soul work that connects us to others, immerses us in God's word, and positions us to grow in grace and mature in Christ. We learn in community.

The practice of *Risk-Taking Mission and Service* involves offering ourselves in purposeful service to others in need,

making a positive difference even at significant personal cost and inconvenience to our own lives. We serve.

Through the practice of *Extravagant Generosity*, we offer our material resources in a manner that supports the causes that transform life and relieve suffering and that enlarges the soul and sustains the spirit. We give back.

These five practices—to receive God's love, to love God in return, to grow in Christ, to serve others, and to give back—are so essential to growth in Christ and to the deepening of the spiritual life that failure to attend to them, develop them, and deepen them with intentionality limits our capacity to live fruitfully and fully, to settle ourselves completely in God, and to become instruments of God's transforming grace. The adjectives—*radical, passionate, intentional, risk-taking,* and *extravagant*—provoke us out of complacency and remind us that these practices require more than haphazard, infrequent, and mediocre attention.

These practices open our heart—to God, to others, to a life that matters, a life rich with meaning, relationship, and contribution. They help us flourish.

Christian Practice

The ministry of Jesus is grounded in personal practices. Jesus' life is marked by prayer, solitude, worship, reflection, the study of scripture, conversation, community, serving, engagement with suffering, and generosity. These personal practices sustained a ministry that opened people to God's grace, transformed human hearts, and changed the circumstances of people in need.

Christian practices are those essential activities we repeat and deepen over time. They create openings for God's spirit to shape us. Practices are not simply principles we talk about; practices are something we do. They make our faith a tangible and visible part of daily life. We see them done in the life of Jesus, and we do them until they become

a way of life for us. We become instruments of God's grace and love.

Through practice, we open ourselves to grace and let ourselves be opened by grace. We follow Christ, step by step, day by day, again and again; and by these steps and through these days, we are changed, we become someone different, we become new creations in Christ.

The books in this series are based on the premise that by repeating and deepening certain fundamental practices, we cooperate with God in our own growth in Christ and participate with the Holy Spirit in our own spiritual maturation. The fundamental practices are rooted in scripture and derived from the clear imperatives of the life of Christ. This isn't a self-improvement, pull-yourself-up-by-your-own-bootstraps notion of how we grow in grace. It's not about trying harder, working longer, or striving more to achieve God's blessing.

The Christian life is a gift of God, an expression of God's grace in Christ, the result of an undeserved and unmerited offering of love toward us. Every step of the journey toward Christ is preceded by, made possible by, and sustained by the perfecting grace of God.

The fruitful life is cultivated by placing ourselves in the most advantageous places to see, receive, learn, and understand the love that has been offered in Christ.

How to Use *The Fruitful Living Series*

The Fruitful Living Series is deeply personal, and as such it is composed of stories—the experiences, hopes, doubts, good efforts, and false starts of people like you and me. Faith journeys are used to illustrate key points so as to encourage honest reflection and conversation. But the approach is not individualistic—only about me, my, and mine. Every experience imbeds us more deeply in the community of Christ because it is in the presence of our sisters and brothers that our spirits are sustained, our hearts encouraged.

I pray for those who reach for these books searching for understanding about their own faith journeys, that it may stimulate them to deeper life in Christ. But I pray especially for those who have been handed these books and who open their pages reluctantly, that they may open themselves to the possibility that something in the stories and reflections

may cause them to think more deeply, pray more earnestly, and serve others in a more fruitful and satisfying way.

This series is experiential rather than systematic or dogmatic. It relies on the experiences of ordinary people who have been extraordinarily shaped by their relationship to God. None of us has the complete picture. Movement toward Christ is never a straight line, uninterrupted, obstacle free, totally consistent, predictable and easily describable. There are no perfect accounts that capture everything that lies behind and no completely reliable maps that outline the future in one's faith journey. Soul work is hard, and following Christ is messy, challenging, joyous, scary, painful, sustaining, and frustratingly indescribable.

This Fruitful Living Series is about the everyday faith of everyday people seeking to listen for God, to love each other, to care for those in need, to embrace the stranger, to live the fruit of the spirit.

These books are practical. They are about what we do daily and intentionally, and about who we become because of how God uses what we do. They suggest a compass rather than map; a direction helpful for many diverse contexts rather than a specific step-by-step, how-to plan that fits only certain terrain.

Engage the material personally. Discover what you can learn about yourself, your relationship with God, your personal desires and internal resistances in the life of faith.

And read *The Fruitful Living Series* with others on the journey to Christ. Use it in house groups, adult Sunday school classes, a weeknight book study, or with your family. Resolve to deepen your own practices of faith. Pray for one another and support one another in Christ. Encourage church leaders and pastors to use the book in retreats, sermon series, or evening studies. These five books focus the essential work that forms disciples; by cultivating these practices in the lives of those reached

by the community of faith, the congregation fulfills its mission of making disciples of Jesus Christ for the transformation of the world.

As a pastor and bishop, I've been granted the privilege of witnessing people whose faith is immeasurably greater than my own, whose sacrifice more than I myself could ever bear, whose impact in the lives of others through their service is immeasurably more than mine, whose personal discipline, depth of spirit, and maturing in Christ is far ahead of anything I shall ever achieve or hope to receive, and whose generosity is so extraordinary that it humbles me completely. This book is about how we learn from their fruitfulness in Christ so that we cooperate with God in becoming what God created us to be.

My prayer for you and your congregation is that *The Fruitful Living Series* helps us all grow in grace and in the knowledge and love of God. May we be changed from the inside out so that we can transform the world for the purposes of Christ.

Growing in Grace

LEARNING IN COMMUNITY

> *Beloved, I do not consider that I*
> *have made it my own; but this one*
> *thing I do: forgetting what lies behind*
> *and straining forward to what lies*
> *ahead, I press on toward the goal for*
> *the prize of the heavenly call of God*
> *in Christ Jesus.*
> *—Philippians 3:13-14*

Rita attends to the last-minute details before people arrive. She sets up the DVD and places her Bible, workbook, and notepad on the recliner in her living room where she will lead tonight's session. As she reviews her notes, Joel starts the coffee maker, mixes lemonade, and sets out cookies he purchased at the bakery on the way home from work. He carries chairs from the dinner table into their living room. With the couch and the other furniture, everyone will have a place, although a few people inevitably prefer to sit on the floor.

Rita and Joel teach an eight-week Bible study focused on the parables of Jesus. Six years earlier, they began their own journey into the exploration of Scripture. They'd been active in the congregation for several months when they responded to an invitation to a series on Philippians. The study stoked their curiosity. Later they belonged to the pastor's Bible study, a weekly series that focused on the Scriptures the pastor used during worship. They enjoyed the refreshing sense of friendship, but wanted something

that delved more deeply. The next year, they joined a Disciple Bible study, an in-depth, long-term study. They weren't sure how the daily readings and the weekly meetings would work, especially with teenagers at home, Rita's career, and Joel's travel; but they tried it anyway. They loved it, and between classes, they found themselves talking about the topics that came up in their readings. They appreciated how closely they were growing to the others in the group. "Belonging to that Bible study was one of the best things we ever did. We began to feel comfortable with the Bible and to feel at home with other people in the congregation."

They continued to participate in Bible studies, usually together as a couple, but sometimes apart. They were surprised and humbled when the pastor asked if they would teach a class themselves. Neither of them has a theological education, and they certainly are no experts in faith matters. The pastor assured them that their task involved facilitating the discussion, helping participants

learn from one another, following the resource outline, and learning to explore Scripture together. They attended a two-hour training, and then agreed to teach the class and to host it in their home.

An interesting mix of people signed up for their house group: A thirty-something, new-to-the-church accountant comes with her friend who lives in her apartment complex; a physician and his wife who works at home with Mom duties; a woman who works as a bank vice-president; a younger couple who are both teachers; another dual-career couple with technology backgrounds; and a recently divorced man employed at a sporting goods store.

With everything ready, folks begin to gather, welcoming one another, catching up, getting their snacks, finding their places. An air of comfort has emerged after only a few weeks together and there are handshakes and embraces and good-humored bantering.

Rita opens the meeting with prayer, outlines their time together, and introduces the three parables they will explore from Luke 15. Some have read the Scriptures and the workbook thoroughly, and others have spent less time in preparation, but everyone expresses initial reactions to what they have read. They watch and discuss a ten-minute DVD that corresponds with the workbook, and then Rita moves them through the parables, highlighting key images and offering questions that stimulate discussion. Members have developed a trust that allows intimate reflection. They share easily. While the topic begins with and returns to Scripture repeatedly, the discussion becomes intermixed with stories about friends, news events, personal experiences, concern about relatives. A sense of compassion, an atmosphere of winsomeness, a willingness to listen, and a mysterious and natural intimacy make this time together different from other gatherings, such as staff meetings at work or classrooms at college.

As the evening ends, Joel leads in prayer as people lift concerns: a sister with cancer, a child anxious about school, a youth project at the church, and a controversial election in the community. Afterward, people continue visiting with one another as they leave.

Having a Plan In Mind

This scenario describes a typical Bible study that includes some of the key elements that mark a wide variety of small-group gatherings—a focus on faith and Scripture, a sense of community, the sharing of prayer. Some meet on Sunday mornings and others on weekday nights; some studies last six weeks and others continue for decades; some are formal, structured, and driven by lessons and resources while others are freestyle and unstructured. Some groups meet in church classrooms, others in members' living rooms, and others in workplace offices or at schools. Growing together in Christ takes many forms.

Faith development refers to how we purposefully learn in community outside of worship in order to deepen our faith and to grow in grace and in the knowledge and love of God. It refers to our active cooperation with the Holy Spirit in our own spiritual growth, a maturation we accomplish through belonging to a faith-forming community such as a Bible study, support group, Sunday school class, house group, women's organization, book study, choir, prayer team, or other small group. Faith development also takes place through retreats, camping ministries, seminars, and support groups that apply faithful living to particular contexts and challenges such as parenting, divorce recovery, living with Alzheimer's, and countless other topics. All of these ministries embed us in a community that helps us to mature in faith and to follow Christ more nearly in our daily living.

BY PREARRANGEMENT WITH MYSELF

How do you find time for Bible study?
One young professional woman answered,
"By prearrangement with myself. I manage
to do other things on time—go to the
gym, take children to school and to soccer
practice, eat, work. I look at my Bible study
as a support group, a regular appointment
with God's grace. I make it a priority, as if
keeping an appointment with Jesus.

If learning in community fosters faith, why describe the personal practice as Intentional Faith Development?

Many followers of Christ desire and value small-group experiences and have benefited from them in the past, but their participation is haphazard, incidental, and infrequent. A short-term study piques their interest at one point and a few years later they attend a home Bible study. Years pass before they go with friends on a weekend retreat. The pattern lacks thoroughness, frequency, and focus. They never practice with enough depth and consistency to feel comfortable or confident with their spirituality. They dabble in religion without growing in grace. Scripture remains strange, mysterious, impenetrable. They enjoy the fellowship but never appreciate close, long-term bonds that lend a sense of trust, strength, and depth to their relationships with others in the community.

Intentional means having a plan in mind. It refers to our determination to act in a specific manner and our

having a purpose to what we do. Intentional derives from Latin words meaning "to stretch out for, to aim at." Paul describes this yearning for greater fullness when he writes, "straining forward to what lies ahead, I press on toward the goal for the prize of the heavenly call of God in Jesus Christ"(Philippians 3:13-14). We seek the perfect love of Christ, to have in us the mind that was in Christ Jesus.

Intentional ratchets up the commitment and consistency. Those who practice Intentional Faith Development make room in their lives for learning faith. They *plan* to feed their spirits. Learning faith becomes a way of life, a practice that is no longer haphazard and incidental but which is central and important. They *regularly* participate in Bible studies, seminars, or retreats to focus on cultivating the spiritual life. They desire to know God and set themselves to the task of learning God's Word through Scripture. Learning becomes a lifelong priority, and they seek progressively more challenging experiences to deepen their understanding of God. They feed their curiosity.

They desire to mature in Christ and put themselves in the most advantageous situations to do so. Priority, purpose, consistency, persistence, and commitment make faith development *intentional*.

The practice of Intentional Faith Development refers to our purposeful learning in Christian community in order to grow in grace and in the knowledge and love of God.

REFLECTION

Let's see how inventive we can be in ENCOURAGING LOVE *and* HELPING OUT, *not avoiding worshiping together as some do but* SPURRING EACH OTHER ON, *especially as we see the* BIG DAY *approaching.*

—*Hebrews 10:24-25*, The Message

INTENTIONAL means having a plan in mind. It refers to our determination to act in a specific manner and our having a purpose to what we do.

Questions

- When have you belonged to a Bible study or class that was helpful, sustaining, and spiritually satisfying? What qualities of the experience made it so?

- How do you tend to your spiritual growth? How have other people served as a catalyst for your own spiritual growth?

- What's the most advantageous setting or gathering for you to learn with others?

- How intentional are you about belonging to a learning community that deepens your spiritual life?

Prayer

Your hands have made and fashioned me, O Lord. Thank you for deep-spirited friends and for all those people you send to me to share my journey to you.

A SCHOOL FOR LOVE

> *For just as the body is one and has many members, and all the members of the body, though many, are one body, so it is with Christ.*
> —1 Corinthians 12:12

We learn in community because Jesus taught us to learn this way. He weaved people into a community around him and taught them through stories, parables, examples, and by modeling behaviors. What he taught filtered through the conversations, deliberations, and experiences of his followers as their relationship to Jesus formed them.

The practice of learning in community continued during the beginnings of the early church. The second chapter of Acts reports people gathering in home and temple to learn from the disciples. Before written Scriptures, they repeated the stories of Jesus, imprinting his teachings upon their hearts. The community provided a supportive network for testing ideas, gaining from other peoples' experiences, sharing the love of Christ, and holding one another accountable to following Christ.

The spiritual life is never a solitary affair.

John Wesley, founder of Methodism, intentionally organized people into small groups for the study of Scripture, prayer, and to "watch after one another in love."[1] Early Methodists met in societies, classes, and bands. They gathered in homes and workplaces and schools. They inquired after one another's spiritual progress with a supportive intimacy. They shared their doubts and hopes and talked about how they had seen God's grace at work in their lives. They learned to "rejoice with those who rejoice" and to "weep with those who weep" (Romans 12:15). They encouraged one another.

Theologically, Wesley based the class meetings on the sanctifying grace of God. *Sanctification* involves our growing in faith, and how the Holy Spirit works within us to help us mature in Christ. Faith is not like a light switch, on or off. It is a growth process, as we step-by-step mature in grace intentionally following in the way of Jesus.

By the grace of God, we pray that we are closer to God and further along in our following of Christ now than we were five years ago.

And we pray that we will be closer to God and further along in our walk with Christ five years from now than we are today. *Sanctification* means our faith journey has direction, trajectory, purpose, a path. We desire to become more Christ-like. We grow in grace and in the knowledge and love of God.

According to Wesley, the Holy Spirit makes this maturation process possible. However, growth in Christ requires us to cooperate with the Holy Spirit in our own sanctification. We cooperate by placing ourselves in the most advantageous situations for learning God's heart, for walking in Jesus' way, and for remaining faithful in our practice of the spiritual life. A congregation or a community of Christ, such as a Bible study, Sunday school class, or

support group, becomes a "school for love" as we learn to give and receive love, to serve others, and to follow Christ more nearly. Community provides the catalyst for growth in Christ.

SOLITARY RELIGION CANNOT SUBSIST AT ALL

John Wesley organized followers of Christ "methodically" into small groups—chapels, classes, and bands—so that they would intermix with other people and with the Holy Spirit in their Christian journey. They met weekly to inquire after one another in love. Wesley wrote, "Christianity is essentially a social religion; and . . . to turn it into a solitary one, is to destroy it." The spiritual life originates in community and leads to community; we are hard-wired for relationship. In community we discover Christ.

We learn faith in community, not only because Jesus and the New Testament have taught us to learn this way, but also because spirituality cannot be learned alone. Peace, forgiveness, mercy, compassion, hope, gentleness, love, grace, serving—these and many other components of belief and practice are communal in nature. They are social and cannot be learned merely from a book. They become part of us as we practice them with other people. We learn them with friends, teachers, mentors, and fellow travelers on the path with Christ.

And learning in community provides accountability in our walk with Christ. Despite our best intentions and the promises we make to ourselves, our commitment to love God and others often wanes and weakens. When we share the journey with other people, they keep us committed just as we keep them on the path of growth in Christ. Practices are best honed with the help of others. With fellow

followers of Christ comes a sense of accountability that we cannot achieve on our own.

As we follow Christ in the company of other Christians, we implicitly make a public commitment among people we respect and care for and who respect and care for us. Those who share our journey comfort us, provoke us, remind us, sympathize with us, confront us, and pray for us. The Holy Spirit uses them to draw us further along toward Christ.

Work schedules and travel may make regular engagement with community nearly impossible for some people. Supported by community, their faith development takes place mostly in solitude—reading, journaling, searching Scripture, and praying. Even in such circumstances, the Holy Spirit uses other people to prompt and encourage. An entirely solitary religion is an impossible contradiction in the following of Christ.

Growing in Grace

Let's return to Rita and Joel and their Bible study. Look around the living room. An accountant and her friend, two young couples, a bank executive, a doctor and his wife, a divorcé. The reading of Scripture. Workbooks. A short video. Ninety minutes together. Conversation. Prayer. How does the Holy Spirit use these ordinary ingredients to resculpt lives in such extraordinary ways?

An interesting dynamic takes place when we read Scripture and talk about it together with others. Several things happen.

Perspective

Focus on Scripture has the effect of pulling each person out of his or her immediate situation to give a larger view, a slightly more universal perspective. Even if people do not

speak aloud about what they are thinking, a topic such as suffering, fairness, jealousy, forgiveness, peace, patience, or sacrifice inevitably draws each toward a personal experience that they are currently facing. The banker listens and mulls over a personnel issue that causes her stress. The divorcé hears the same conversation and reads the same Scripture, but replays in his mind a conversation with his daughter from the night before. The doctor thinks about the estrangement he feels from his sister; one of the young couples casts a knowing glance at each other as they think of the argument they had earlier in the evening. The Spirit moves where it chooses (John 3:8), and its gentle breeze rustles through the souls of each member of the group.

Amazingly, people from vastly different circumstances can read a parable prayerfully, or hear someone share a personal experience about God's activity, and each feels that the topic strikes the target to address a particular challenge in his or her own life.

WE NEED A NUDGE

Tammy said, "Each time I leave a Bible study session, I feel encouraged to do things I was fearful to do before. We always end up talking each other into things—to speak up at work, to forgive a sister, to visit someone who is grieving. We know these are the right things to do. But we need a nudge." Community fosters accountability. We become the voice of Christ to each other.

The benefit of sifting through Scripture with companions is not merely the acquisition of historical facts, theological theories, or ideas. The benefit cannot be reduced to gleaning helpful hints for living or from the advice our friends give us. Each person learns something relevant to his or her

soul's desire. Like standing on a balcony looking down from above at all our interactions with others, each person receives a wider perspective on the world in which they work, love, play, and serve. As meaning is unlocked by one person on a topic, an overflowing of insight connects to other persons at an interior level beyond conscious awareness. What we learn may be inexpressible with complete awareness. The Spirit of God works through the conversation, weaving, binding, penetrating, healing, provoking, correcting, reminding, reconciling.

And by the grace of God, with frequent and consistent participation in the faith community, various spiritually sustaining attributes are deepened, and people find themselves with more courage, more patience, a greater compassion, a deeper sense of fairness, a higher commitment to fidelity, more resolve, more peace. The transformation may be gradual, but it is significant and life-changing. Like a potter forming clay, God gently and persistently shapes us.

The fruit of Intentional Faith Development is not merely to know more *about* God but to *know* God, to see through the *idea* of God to God himself. Spiritual knowledge arises in us in mysterious ways. A memorable insight is mulled over and replayed dozens of times during the week that follows a Bible study. We think of it as we wait at the stoplight on the way to the grocery store, it comes to mind as we ride the subway to work, it surfaces during a staff meeting at the office or during dinner with family. Spiritual knowledge is not information we apply to a problem that provides the solution; it's not like a number we plug into a formula that solves everything. Rather, a new awareness takes root; a new perception is formed; a new confidence is discovered; a new connection made; or a new hope recovered that changes how we think, feel, and act. The impact is real, and with the continued practice of spiritual exploration, we experience an increasing benefit, a greater openness to grace, a more refined shaping of ourselves by God. We begin to know God more intimately.

Knowing God, with time, mysteriously causes us to become a different kind of person, with more depth, peace, and courage. We become more hopeful, more thankful, less reactive, gentler, more patient, more resilient, less angry, better able to relate. Sometimes the differences are nuanced and the progress feels imperceptibly slow, like someone taking yoga classes who appears the same from the outside, but who has developed within them a greater flexibility, smoother breathing, and increased circulation. The change is real, but hardly discernible by other people at first. Other times, the change noticeably reshapes outward behaviors. Slow or fast, unrevealed or dramatic—knowing God changes us from the inside out. We follow Christ more closely.

REFLECTION

REJOICE
with those who
REJOICE,
WEEP
with those who
WEEP.

—*Romans 12:15*

Peace, forgiveness, mercy, compassion, hope, gentleness, love, grace, serving—these are communal in nature. They are social and cannot be learned merely from a book. They become part of us as we practice them with other people.

The Practice of Intentional Faith Development

Questions

- How do you tend to your spiritual growth? How have other people served as a catalyst for your own spiritual growth?

- What people are most instrumental in your faith development today, and how?

- What are a few ways that you are a different person from what you might have been because you have belonged to a faith community?

Prayer

Teach me to do your will, for you are my God. Change me from the inside out.

Growing in Grace

A MEANS OF GRACE

All scripture is inspired by God and is useful for teaching, for reproof, for correction, and for training in righteousness.
—*2 Timothy 3:16*

Spiritual Awareness

Focused learning opens the spiritual world to us and stimulates an attentiveness that helps us see elements of soul and grace we might never have noticed before.

Some years ago, I spotted what I thought was an unusually beautiful and rare bird near my home. After searching bird guide books, I discovered that the strikingly colorful bird was actually quite common in my area. After I saw it once, I began to see it regularly. I had long enjoyed an active outdoor life that included camping, hiking, kayaking, and fishing; and I could not believe that I had never noticed this bird before. Spotting this bird permanently changed me. I wondered what else I was missing, and I bought a pair of binoculars, a field guide to birds, and became a birder.

With a new intentionality, I began to read about birds and talk with birders. My eyes and my attitude were

now attuned to birds, and with training and experience I began to see them everywhere—unusual birds, striking in their colors and behaviors, were living in my own backyard. I learned where and how to look—on the ground, in the bushes, along the roadsides, under the eaves of buildings. I learned their habits—the shy ones and the boisterous, the flamboyant and the modest. I saw birds I would have overlooked before, noticing them in places I wasn't aware existed. Prior to my "conversion," seeing birds was accidental and unintentional for me; I couldn't discern distinctions, didn't know their names, and had little appreciation for them. Beyond the most ordinary and common, they were unseen and unknown to me. With intentionality, I began to see the world around me from a different perspective, aware of the unseen enchanted world of migration, of nest-building and foraging. I now love birds, and bird books line my shelves and bird drawings adorn my walls. My eyes have been opened to a whole new world.

In the same way, when we open Scripture, belong to a community of Christ, and start to explore life with God, we detect God's presence and activity that we never before noticed. A new world opens. We learn a new vocabulary. With soul work, an unseen world that we never knew existed becomes visible. Regular Bible study with others brings topics before us that we otherwise overlook, and we learn to identify them with greater clarity. We learn to see God.

Jesus came "to open the eyes of the blind" (Luke 4:18). As we delve into Scripture, we look afresh at our family life, our work world, our inner life, and the world around us. When we notice how the Spirit moves, we perceive signs of grace. We identify inner attitudes, emotions, and experiences that inhibit growth and happiness—envy, pride, guilt, anger. Hope, joy, forgiveness, service, spirit, grace—these and other elements of faith become visible and tangible. Questions that previously seemed elusive or unimportant become real: How have I experienced God in

the past week? How has God sustained me, reminded me, or called me? How is God at work in my life?

Without intentionally cultivating faith, we go through life self-blinded, seeing only a portion of what is before us. We perceive the world through cultural filters that make it nearly impossible to see what is really most important. Whole worlds exist right before us, including the world of spirit, the God-related life, the presence and work of Christ. Learning in community opens our eyes.

Spiritual Sustenance

Belonging to a learning faith community provides companionship that sustains us through difficult experiences. Nothing is as disheartening as a lonely struggle. Many communities and congregations are too large for people to know others well, and so it's in the intimacy of small groups—classes, Bible studies, choirs, prayer groups—that we learn each others' names, pray for one another, and learn to care for one another. Christian companions become

the people God uses to sustain us through the ordinary ups and downs of living, and also through those times of extraordinary darkness and grief.

As we pray for one another, community lifts away what obstructs hope. Belonging tempers grief so that it doesn't break us but heals us and makes us stronger. Interwoven into a community, we discover a place of trust, of safety, of love. We feel connected. And that makes all the difference during times of doubt, suffering, or loss. Communion with one another deepens our communion to God.

"I don't know how I would have made it through these last two years without my friends from church." I've heard that repeated by people recovering from grief or simply navigating the ordinary challenges of life. They describe a healthy interdependence rather than an unhealthy dependence or self-deluded independence; they speak of lives interwoven by the grace of God. They describe the benefit of belonging.

The thread of life is fragile. A few cells within a healthy body grow erratically and we receive the diagnosis of cancer; a second's misjudgment at an intersection, and a life is lost; a heart that keeps its cadence for decades skips a few beats and we find ourselves in intensive care; a friend loses her baby during pregnancy; an aging parent shows signs of Alzheimer's; violence strikes someone we know. None of us is immune to such devastating experiences for ourselves, our families, or among our friends. Inexpressible suffering barges in at unexpected moments. And everyone balances the more common (yet anguishing) anxieties, setbacks, and losses that challenge our ability to cope—conflict at home, financial loss, trouble with teenagers, struggles with alcohol, feelings of loneliness. No one lives without facing a threatening darkness.

We overestimate our capacity to handle these things all by ourselves, and we underestimate the power of community to help. Belonging to a caring community, we discover a sustenance that does not answer all our questions or end all our challenges, but which keeps us connected, rooted,

grounded. When the worst happens, God doesn't promise us an answer; God provides us a relationship. Through sustaining relationships, we discover that God is not aloof from life and disinterested in us. Instead, God gets in the trenches and suffers with us. We are not alone. God is with us. God's presence reaches us through the people who love us. The thread of life is fragile, but the fabric of life is eternal.

Belonging to a supportive community provides an interpretive context that helps us understand our experience with greater clarity and hopefulness. Perhaps we can't stop the progress of cancer, but in Christian community we find a place to go for refuge, strength, peace, meaning, and hope. Stories from Scripture, mutual prayer, and receiving the embrace of others help us move from one place in our soul to another, from despair to hope, from death to life. We more ably integrate our sufferings into

a meaningful narrative that helps us get through the day. Belonging deepens hope; love creates trust; prayer lends strength. A threatening darkness becomes a nourishing darkness with patches of sunlight. We develop resilience as our faith helps us assimilate circumstances that result from events we would never choose. No one can survive significant loss well without being part of a community that cares. Sustained by faith, mortality becomes a catalyst for living more joyfully, intensely, and purposefully. In Christ, by love given and love received, we practice death and resurrection, and we rehearse the continuing narrative of God's grace, creation, and new birth. We flourish.

By ourselves, any one of the challenges that beset us can paralyze us, cause us to become stuck, disconnected, dead. When all that lies ahead vanishes from view, an unassailable hopelessness arises. Community pulls us out of ourselves and carries us toward God.

I remember visiting a woman whose husband had died a few months before. Her friends were concerned because she would never leave the house. She sat in her rocking chair in her living room from morning to evening. In front of her rested the urn that contained her husband's ashes. With his death, her life ended. Every day was spent sitting in her chair focusing on her loss. With continued contact, we convinced her to see a doctor. We began to reconnect her to community, to cast threads to re-bind her to friends and neighbors. People reached for her, and slowly she began to respond. She became part of a women's Bible study, and eventually began to help with projects around the church. Slowly she emerged a new person. Some months later, I visited again. The rocking chair now faced a window with a phone beside it. Letters she was addressing for a church project were scattered on the coffee table. The urn rested on a shelf above the fireplace, still present but no longer the focal point of her existence.

This example has become symbolic for me. Jesus confronted the person paralyzed beside the pool for thirty-eight years with the question, "Do you want to be made well?" (John 5:6). In the gloom of grief, depression, loss, and pain, the answer is not simple. Belonging to a faith community helps us to enfold our past into the present and future, to integrate suffering into a coherent understanding of who we are today and what God intends for our future. Community helps us to flow on, and in the flowing on, hope begins to kill the deadness in our souls.

Moral Resolve

God also uses community to save us from ourselves and the self-destructive choices we make. Some hardships result from our own massive mistakes, painful misjudgments, and harmful behavior. When we face temptations beyond what we can bear, our friends in Christ reinforce our resolve, strengthen our covenants, and remind us of the

critical commitments that bind us. Discussing a passage in Scripture about jealousy, hate, lust, pride, or greed may indirectly address temptations and fears that are far too real and risky to share aloud. Mulling over a Scripture's meaning addresses things diagonally rather than head on, and allows us to contemplate significant issues we otherwise avoid. Bringing such soul work into conscious awareness provides us our best chance to reassess and make good decisions.

Acknowledging the power of temptation and sin, naming them, and exploring them fosters a humility that helps us to restrain ourselves or amend destructive impulses. A thin spirituality that is untested and uncorrected by community leads to self-deception; in honest community, we recognize our incredible capacity to delude ourselves. Jesus says, "Where two or three or gathered in my name, I am there among them" (Matthew 18:20). Christ's voice, in our sisters and brothers, brings us back to ourselves, sustains us, and

heals us. In the gift of community we discover the power of confession and of forgiveness, and we find the strength to turn around before it is too late and to change direction even after harm is done. Friends keep us from falling, and when we fall, they pick us up.

Spiritual Encouragement

In community we catch the contagious quality of faith and hope. Gathering stokes the flames of each member of the group. We encourage one another. (*Encourage* literally means 'to put courage into, to give heart!') We become more in Christ because of the influence of friends. We talk one another into things. We take bolder action that we might otherwise avoid. We follow Christ more eagerly.

Tim worked as a financial officer of a mid-sized business. After his first year, he began to feel uneasy within himself about his job.

The owners skated close to the edge of acceptable ethical practice, and increasingly Tim felt uncomfortable with their style. During this period, every Bible study Tim attended seemed to be about his situation. During prayer time with his friends, he found himself contemplating what he ought to do. His faith community gave him a vocabulary for understanding what was going on inside, and it gave him the courage to finally speak with his wife about his uneasiness and then to seek the counsel of trusted friends. Without his growing familiarity with the interior life, Tim might never have identified the values that he held that conflicted with the corporate culture. He resigned amicably from his job and moved to another company. Later, his previous employers were accused of major ethical violations. "I just knew it was wrong for my soul," Tim says. "I was struggling with something. It was intuitive and internal, but it was real. Without the friends and the Bible study, I would never have acted." Following Christ educates the heart.

THE ONE I FEED

From a Native American faith tradition we receive the story of a grandfather telling his grandchild about spiritual struggle and growth. "Inside me there are two wolves that fight each other all the time. One is motivated by peace, gentleness, honesty, justice, and love. The other lives by resentment, bitterness, hate, anger, and violence." "Which one wins?" asks the child. "The one I feed," answers the elder.

This resonates with Paul's admonition to feed the new nature and starve the old (Romans 13:14). Intentional Faith Development feeds the new creation.

Mutual Care

In community we practice caring for one another. We discover what it feels like to be genuinely prayed for, to have others invest themselves in our well-being, to have confidants who care about what happens to us. In the love others show us, we catch a partial and imperfect glimpse of the complete and unconditional love God has for us. Our burdens are not ours to bear entirely on our own. Our lives become intermingled. By sharing Christ, we share life.

Growth results not merely from what we do, but most especially from *what God does*. Opening ourselves to Scripture, praying for one another, and caring for one another are concrete and personal ways God reaches into our lives to work for our well-being. God uses the stories of countless generations recorded in Scripture and the experiences and love of our friends to sculpt our souls. Our participation invites the Holy Spirit to cooperate with

us in the perfecting of our love. Talking and praying and laughing and learning create a dynamic that lifts Jesus' teachings off the printed page and puts them into daily practice. The Bible comes alive, a letter from God, the source of assurance, belonging, and invitation. God works through community.

God has hard-wired us for belonging; learning how to give and receive love is an essential element of human existence and the key to flourishing. Community is the way God feeds our spirits. Jesus said, "I am the vine, you are the branches" (John 15:5). As we stay connected to Christ, we thrive; disconnected, we wither. Community is God's way of bringing us Christ.

The Bible, a DVD, a workbook, conversation, prayer, an unusual assortment of people—what comes of it? Christ. Strength. Life. Learning in community is a means of grace, and it changes our lives.

REFLECTION

ASK, *and it will be given you;*
  SEARCH, *and you will find;*
    KNOCK, *and the door will be*
      OPENED *for you.*
For everyone who asks RECEIVES,
  and everyone who searches FINDS,
    and for everyone who KNOCKS,
      the door will be OPENED.

—Matthew 7:7-8

When we open Scripture, belong to a community of Christ, and start to explore life with God, we detect God's presence and activity that we never before noticed.

Questions

- What keeps you aware of the spiritual dimension in your daily life?
- What are you curious about in the spiritual life, and how do you explore faith?
- How have you seen God at work in the world during the past week? How does belonging to a faith community help you see God in new ways?
- When has belonging to a community of faith helped you with a significant life decision or challenge? How did God work through the community?
- How does listening for God help you listen to others? How does listening to others help you listen for God?

Prayer

Cultivate in me a life of wonder, faith, love, steadiness, and service. The life to which you call me, may I embrace it fervently and forever.

CULTIVATING THE SPIRITUAL LIFE

For where two or three are gathered in my name, I am there among them.
—*Matthew 18:20*

If Intentional Faith Development provides such rich spiritual benefits, what keeps us from participating? Why do we resist?

People who have never belonged to a Bible study or adult class hesitate because they fear feeling inadequate or embarrassed by their lack of familiarity with Scripture or with religious terms. They don't know what happens in a class or what will be expected of them. What if someone asks them a question they don't know how to answer? Will they be called upon to pray aloud? They don't know what kind of Bible to bring to the class. They wonder whether they will be accepted. Those who are familiar with the rhythm of small-group spiritual exploration forget how intimidating it is for newcomers. It takes courage and a willingness to handle the awkwardness to break into any new learning situation—Bible study, tennis lessons, or knitting classes. Are we willing to experience the feeling of "temporary incompetence" in order to attain a sense of confidence?

And people resist because they don't know the other people who might be present. It's hard to walk into a room of strangers, wondering whether we will get along with them or whether they will accept us. Will someone dominate the conversations or intimidate others? Will people be impatient with us? How will others react if I disagree? People usually find it easier to join a group when they go along with someone they already know so that they have someone to support them and to talk about the experience with afterward.

With schedules filled up with work and family obligations, many people simply cannot find time to attend a weekly gathering. In fantasy-like fashion, they await the day when something suddenly changes and they finally have time to nourish their spirit. But no one ever *finds* time; they *make* time. They move other important things around in their schedules and they commit. They decide growing in Christ has such significant impact on other aspects of their living that it's worth making the time.

IT'S NOTICEABLE

Concert musician Ignacy Paderewski tells about how he continues to practice every day, even after years of focused learning. "If I miss one day of practice," he says, "I notice it. If I miss two days, the critics notice it. If I miss three days, the audience notices it."

Neglect our feeding the Spirit for a few days, and we sense the difference. Something feels unsettled. Avoid it for several days, and our family notices. Neglect the spiritual life for too long, and even those who know us from a distance—neighbors and co-workers—begin to notice.

Sometimes people resist participation because they do not believe all the same things that others in the group believe. I belonged to a Bible study once that was led by

someone whose theology was radically different from my own. Honestly, I didn't believe much of what I heard the teacher say, and my faith expression differed considerably from others in the group. Nevertheless, many of the insights shared by others deeply touched me and stimulated me to delve deeper in my own reflection. My relationship with God deepened even though I disagreed with many of the teacher 's lessons.

And some people resist participation in an ongoing class because they want the fastest, cheapest, and least transformational route to the spiritual life. They think that merely reading a best-selling book, watching a television broadcast, or following a few simple steps will bring them long-lasting happiness. The prospect of sustained practice, learning, growing, and maturing puts them off. They want quick fixes.

God desires a relationship with us. God wants us to experience the riches of God's grace. When we cooperate

with God by placing ourselves in Christian community, we make ourselves more able to absorb God's truth. When we remain too busy or too resistant, God's attempts to reach us are like a pencil on glass and we remain unchanged.

The inner world is a source of power and strength, but it needs to be cultivated. We do so through the practice of Intentional Faith Development.

The Practice of Intentional Faith Development

People who practice Intentional Faith Development commit themselves to learning the faith and growing in grace. They overcome excuses, make time, find a learning community that fits their schedule, and commit to it. They delve deeper.

They find a way to learn that fits their own temperament and learning style. They experiment and explore until

something works that sustains their spiritual curiosity and growth in Christ. They persist until they find what's right for them. They learn how to learn.

They consciously avoid the temptation to make scriptural exploration abstract and detached from life. They ask, "What is God reminding me of in this message? What is God inviting me to do, challenging me to learn, or calling me to change?" They connect God to life.

They participate less as a consumer of religion and more as a cultivator of the spiritual life. They don't expect all things to be provided for them. They resist being spoon-fed or merely seeking quick tips or instant success. They internalize life with Christ. They cultivate spiritual life.

People who value Intentional Faith Development teach their children to learn about spiritual matters. They enroll them in children's choirs, Sunday school classes, or vacation Bible school. They talk with their children about what they

learn. They cultivate a home atmosphere that encourages faith practices and rewards inquisitiveness, curiosity, and exploration of the spiritual life. They share wonder and honor the enchantment and mystery of life. They make their homes a place of affection where God's love is felt and God's grace is named. They teach faith.

They enjoy much laughter and more love. A learning group becomes a place to relax rather than to tense up. Group dynamics are flexible rather than fragile, and people feel free to be themselves. Laughter is part of the music of faith and tears are the soul's release. They laugh with those who laugh and weep with those who weep.

People who practice Intentional Faith Development avail themselves of increasingly more challenging learning opportunities. They ask themselves, "What am I learning now that is different from an earlier age?" They stretch.

Supported by community, they develop faith in solitude by reading, reflection, and prayer. They carve out time to

invite the Spirit in. They create an open, attentive, gracious environment where the Spirit doesn't mind showing up.

They need community as much as they need air. They pray for one another, stay in touch, follow-up, express sympathy, and practice compassion. They love people without needing to fully understand them. They rescue one another from the self-absorption that drains something essential from the soul. They love enough to gently correct. They sustain with a word. Care for others heals their own souls.

They've learned that if you don't repeatedly plow the earth, the ground becomes so hard that nothing new can grow and no seeds can take root. In each season they recommit to some form of study or class or retreat. They open themselves anew to insight. They become resilient, adaptable, and malleable rather than fixed, stagnant, and impenetrable.

People who grow in grace realize that if they follow Christ for a thousand years, they will still need to learn as much on the last day as on the first. The sanctifying grace of God never ceases.

Through the practice of Radical Hospitality, we open ourselves to receiving God's love. We say *Yes* to God. Through Passionate Worship, we love God in return, offering our hearts to God to create us anew. Through the practice of Intentional Faith Development, we grow in grace and in the knowledge and love of God. As we delve more deeply into the spiritual life, we cannot help but perceive God calling us to make a positive difference in the lives of people around us, and this takes us to the next practice, Risk-Taking Mission and Service.

REFLECTION

Friends, don't get me wrong:
BY NO MEANS *do I count myself*
AN EXPERT *in all of this,*
where GOD *is beckoning us*
ONWARD - TO JESUS.
I'M OFF *and* RUNNING,
and I'M NOT TURNING BACK.

—*Philippians 3:13-14 The Message*

The inner world is a source
of power and strength, but it
needs to be cultivated.
We do so through the practice of
Intentional Faith Development.

Questions

- What keeps you from developing a more consistent pattern of learning faith in community?
- How do you cooperate with God in your own spiritual growth? How do the patterns of your life limit God's ability to work within you?
- Who provides spiritual encouragement for you? For whom do you provide spiritual encouragement?
- When have you been encouraged by friends in the faith community to follow Christ more closely, eagerly, or boldly?
- What kind of person do you hope to be ten years from now in your following of Christ? What patterns or practices will help you get there?

Prayer

By your Spirit, weave me into the fabric of faith, build me into the body of Christ, create in me a sense of belonging and connection to you through other people.

Leader Helps
for Small Group Sessions

Growing in Grace

SESSION 1: *Learning in Community*

Focus Point: Intentional Faith Development is purposefully learning in community in order to deepen our faith and grow in grace and in the knowledge and love of God.

GETTING READY *(Prior to the Session)*

- Read Chapter 1 in Growing in Grace: The Practice of Intentional Faith Development.
- Write the key Scripture and focus point on a board or chart.
- Review Digging In and Making Application, and select the points and discussion questions you will cover.
- Acquire a box of index cards and a bag of pens.
- Pray for the session and for your group members.

Key Scripture: *Beloved, I do not consider that I have made it my own; but this one thing I do: forgetting what lies behind and straining forward to what lies ahead, I press on toward the goal for the prize of the heavenly call of God in Christ Jesus. Philippians 3:13-14*

Main Ideas:

- Intentional Faith Development is purposefully learning in community outside of worship in order to deepen our faith and to grow in grace and in the knowledge and love of God.
- *Faith development* refers to how we purposefully learn in community outside of worship in order to deepen our faith and grow in grace and in the knowledge and love of God. It refers to our active cooperation with the Holy Spirit in our own spiritual growth through belonging to a faith-forming community such as Bible study, Sunday school class, house group, women's organization, or other small group.
- *Intentional* means having a plan in mind. It refers to our determination to act in a specific manner and our having a purpose to what we do. *Intentional* ratchets up the commitment and consistency.
- Those who practice Intentional Faith Development make room in their lives for learning faith.

GETTING STARTED

Opening Prayer

O God, your plan is for us to continue maturing in faith throughout life, and you invite us to actively cooperate with the Holy Spirit in this process. Help us to make room in our lives for learning faith, and give us the commitment and consistency we need to overcome the obstacles. In Jesus' name we pray. Amen.

Growing in Grace

DIGGING IN

Read the excerpt from Chapter 1 that begins, "Faith development refers to how we purposefully learn in community outside of worship in order to deepen our faith and to grow in grace and in the knowledge and love of God" (p. 23).

Group Discussion
• Why do you think spiritual growth requires our active cooperation with the Holy Spirit?
• Why do you think belonging to a faith-forming community is an important part of this process?
• When have you belonged to a Bible study, class, or other group that helped you to mature in faith and to follow Christ more closely? How would you describe your experience in this faith-forming community?

Ask someone to read aloud Philippians 3:13-14.

Group Discussion
• How was "intentional" defined in the chapter?
• Why do you think it is important to be intentional about faith development?
• How do you make room in your life for faith development?
• How are you intentional about feeding your spirit?

MAKING APPLICATION

What Does It Look Like?
Review the experience of Rita and Joel from Chapter 1. Share these points with the group :
-Their faith development began in small group Bible studies and then deeper studies.
-They now host and lead a Bible study in their home.
-Their meeting consists of Bible study, video teaching, discussion, and prayer.
-The group shares experiences and concerns with a deeper level of intimacy and vulnerability.

Briefly discuss
• Why is meeting together like Rita and Joel's group important in order to grow in faith?
• What is required of us to participate in such a group?

Read aloud the following passage from Chapter 1, By Prearrangement With Myself (p. 24).

Hand out note cards and pens to each participant. Ask them to write the following questions along with their answers on their note cards. These answers will not be shared, but encourage them to keep this card in their Bibles or books and bring them each week as they will add to the list.

• What is your current level of intentionality when it comes to your faith development?
• What is standing in the way of going deeper?

What Now?
Instruct participants to reflect silently in response to this question:
• In light of all we have shared today, what do you sense God saying to you?

End by inviting answers to these questions:
In response, what will you do differently this week?
How will what you learned this week change how you live your life?

Close your session with prayer requests and invite a participant to close in prayer.

SESSION 2: *A School for Love*

Focus Point: We learn in community because Jesus and the New Testament have taught us to learn this way, and because spirituality cannot be learned alone.

GETTING READY *(Prior to the Session)*

Key Scripture: *For just as the body is one and has many members, and all the members of the body, though many, are one body, so it is with Christ. I Corinthians 12: 12*

Main Ideas:
- We learn in community because Jesus and the New Testament have taught us to learn this way, and because spirituality cannot be learned alone.
- Learning in community provides accountability in our walk with Christ.
- Community, such as a Bible study or support group, becomes a "school of love" as we learn to give and receive love, to serve others, and to follow Christ more nearly. Community provides the catalyst for growth in Christ.

GETTING STARTED

Opening Prayer
O God, your plan is for us to grow in faith throughout our lives. We know we grow in faith through belonging to a community that helps us to grow in grace and in the knowledge and love of God. Help us overcome schedules and distractions to make the time to learn in a community of faith. In Jesus' name we pray. Amen.

DIGGING IN

Read the two paragraph passage from Chapter 2 that begins, "We learn in community because Jesus taught us to learn this way " (p. 32).
Group Discussion
- How did Jesus model and teach the practice of learning in community?
- How did the early church continue the practice of learning in community?
- What were some of the benefits of this practice?

Emphasize the importance of community to spiritual growth by making the following statements:
- "The spiritual life is never a solitary affair."
- "Community provides the catalyst for growth in Christ."
- Then read the passage titled, "Solitary Religion Cannot Subsist at All" (p. 35).

Group Discussion
- Why do you think community is critical to the spiritual life?
- How has community been a catalyst for your own spiritual growth?
- How have you "discovered Christ" in community?

Read aloud the excerpt from Chapter 2 that begins, "The benefit of sifting through Scripture with companions is not merely the acquisition of facts . . ." (p. 40).
- What are the benefits of growing in grace in community with other believers?
- How does the Spirit of God work through our faith communities to help us grow?

MAKING APPLICATION

What Does It Look Like?
Read aloud the excerpt titled, "We Need a Nudge" (p. 40).
Briefly discuss:
- When has the Spirit nudged you in a small group or Bible study?
- When has God used to you nudge someone in your group?

Wrap up the session by reading aloud the following passage from Chapter 2:
"The fruit of Intentional Faith Development is not merely to know more *about* God but to *know* God, to see through the *idea* of God to God himself. Spiritual knowledge arises in us in mysterious ways . . . . The impact is real, and with the continued practice of spiritual exploration, we experience an increasing benefit, a greater openness to grace, a more refined shaping of ourselves by God. We being to know God more intimately . . . . Knowing God, with time, mysteriously causes us to become a different kind of person, with more depth, peace, and courage. We become more hopeful, more thankful, less reactive, gentler, more patient, more resilient, less angry, better able to relate."

Invite the group to write two new questions along with their answers on their note cards. These answers will not be shared, but encourage them to keep this card in their Bibles or books and bring them each week as they will add to the list.
• How are you growing in grace right now?
• How could you become more intentional about your faith development?

What Now?
Instruct participants to reflect silently in response to this question:
• In light of all we have shared today, what do you sense God saying to you?

End by inviting answers to these questions:
• In response, what will you do differently this week?
• How will what you learned this week change how you live your life?

Close your session with prayer requests and invite a participant to close in prayer.

SESSION 3: *A Means of Grace*

Focus Point: When we practice intentional faith development, we are changed from the inside out as we come to know God more intimately and follow Christ more closely.

GETTING READY *(Prior to the Session)*

Key Scripture: *All scripture is inspired by God and is useful for teaching, for reproof, for correction, and for training in righteousness. 2 Timothy 3:16*

Main Ideas:
- When we open Scripture, belong to a community of Christ, and start to explore life with God, we detect God's presence and activity that we never before noticed.
- Belonging to a learning faith community provides companionship that sustains us through difficult experiences.
- In community we catch the contagious quality of faith and hope and we practice caring for one another.

GETTING STARTED

Opening Prayer
Gracious God, Cultivate in us a life of wonder, faith, love, steadiness, and service. Help us to grow in our faith each day. The life to which you call us, may we embrace it fervently and forever. In Jesus' name we pray. Amen.

DIGGING IN

Read aloud the two paragraph passage from Chapter 3 beginning with, "In the same way, when we open Scripture, belong to a community of Christ, and start to explore life with God, we detect God's presence and activity that we never before noticed" (p. 50).
Group Discussion
- How has regular Bible study with others "opened your eyes"?
- What keeps you aware of the spiritual dimension in your life? How have you learned to see God in fresh ways?
- Many communities and congregations are too large for people to know others well, it is in the intimacy of small groups that we come to feel connected. Point out that all

of us experience challenges and difficulties in life—from common set- backs to more devastating losses.
- Share this point for emphasis: "Belonging to a caring community, we discover a sustenance that does not answer all our questions or end all our challenges, but which keeps us connected, rooted, grounded."

Group Discussion
- When was a time when you or a member of your group helped sustain another person during a time of difficulty or grief? What did you learn about yourself through the experience? What did you learn about Christ?
- Why do you think communion with one another deepens our communion to God?
- Describe a time when you were encouraged (whether directly or indirectly) by friends in a faith community to follow Christ more closely, eagerly, or boldly.

MAKING APPLICATION

What Does It Look Like?
Read the following excerpt from Chapter 3 beginning, " I remember visiting a woman whose husband had died a few months before" (p. 56).

Briefly discuss
- How did becoming part of a faith community change this woman?

Invite participants to pull out their note cards from last week. Ask them to write two new questions along with their answers on their note cards. These answers will not be shared, but encourage them to keep this card in their Bibles or books and bring them each week as they will add to the list.
- How closely are connected to the vine today?
- How will you connect to Christ through community?

What Now?
Instruct participants to reflect silently in response to this question:
- In light of all we have shared today, what do you sense God saying to you?

End by inviting answers to these questions:
- In response, what will you do differently this week?
- How will what you learned this week change how you live your life?

Close your session with prayer requests and invite a participant to close in prayer

SESSION 4: *Cultivating the Spiritual Life*
Focus Point: People who practice Intentional Faith Development commit themselves to learning the faith and growing in grace.

GETTING READY *(Prior to the Session)*

Key Scripture: *For where two or three are gathered in my name, I am there among them. Matthew 18: 20*

Main Ideas:
• To practice Intentional Faith Development, people must overcome excuses, make time, find a learning community that fits their schedule, and commit themselves to it.
• People who practice Intentional Faith Development are cultivators of the spiritual life as opposed to consumers of religion. They experiment and explore until they find what works of them, and they continually stretch and challenge themselves to reach new levels of growth.

GETTING STARTED

Opening Prayer
O, God, Help us to continue to grow every day and every year. Teach us the usefulness of your Word—showing us life-truths, exposing our rebellion, correcting our misjudgments,and training me in Jesus' way. In Jesus' name we pray. Amen.

DIGGING IN

Acknowledge that there are many obstacles or resistances to Intentional Faith Development. Invite participants to skim Chapter 4 and call out any obstacles to faith development they can find.
Group Discussion
• What has kept you from pursuing or practicing Intentional Faith Development in the past?
• How did you overcome these obstacles?
• Why are we prone to wanting a "quick fix" instead of a deep exploration of spiritual things?

Acknowledge that Intentional Faith Development requires commitment and persistence and must be tailored to fit the learning style and temperament of the individual. Ask the group to highlight the habits of those who practice Intentional Faith Development from the chapter.

Group Discussion
• When it comes to Intentional Faith Development, what fits your temperament and learning style? What works for you?
• What are you curious about in the spiritual life at this time? what are you doing to explore faith more deeply?
• Which items on the list need attention in your life?
• Which items on the list mark a sense of growth in your faith development?

MAKING APPLICATION

What Does It Look Like?
Read aloud this paragraph from Chapter 4, titled It's Noticeable (p. 70).
Briefly discuss
• How does our lack of intentional faith development began to show in our daily lives—to ourselves, to God, and to others?

Invite participants to pull out their note cards from last week. Ask them to write two new questions along with their answers on their note cards. These answers will not be shared, but encourage them to keep this card in their Bibles or books and bring them each week as they will add to the list.
• What is your current plan for intentional faith development?
• What steps can you take to delve deeper?

What Now?
Instruct participants to reflect silently in response to this question:
• In light of all we have shared today, what do you sense God saying to you?

End by inviting answers to these questions:
• In response to these sessions on Intentional Faith Development, what will you do differently this week?
• How will what you learned this week and in the book Growing in Grace: The Practice of Intentional Faith Development. change how you live your life?

Close your session with prayer requests and invite a participant to close in prayer.

Notes

1 Wesley, Vol. 8, "A Plain Account of the People Called Methodists"; p. 260, paraphrased.

Growing in Grace
The Practice of
Intentional Faith Development

Let us consider how to provoke one another to love and good deeds, not neglecting to meet together, as is the habit of some, but encouraging one another . . . —Hebrews 10:24-25

_____

_____

_____

_____

_____

_____

_____

_____

_____

_____

_____

_____

_____

Growing in Grace

The Practice of
Intentional Faith Development

Let us consider how to provoke one another to love and good deeds, not neglecting to meet together, as is the habit of some, but encouraging one another . . . —Hebrews 10:24-25

Growing in Grace
The Practice of
Intentional Faith Development

Let us consider how to provoke one another to love and good deeds, not neglecting to meet together, as is the habit of some, but encouraging one another . . . —Hebrews 10:24-25

Growing in Grace

The Practice of
Intentional Faith Development

Let us consider how to provoke one another to love and good deeds, not neglecting to meet together, as is the habit of some, but encouraging one another . . . —Hebrews 10:24-25

_____

_____

_____

_____

_____

_____

_____

_____

_____

_____

_____

_____